Walks with

AROUND
CONISTON

Ron Bickerton

A **QUESTA** Guide

© Ron Bickerton 2005

ISBN 1 898808 19 8

PUBLISHER'S NOTE

It is the responsibility of parents when out walking with children to supervise them and to make judgements about whether any part of a walk is unsuitable for them.

Readers are advised that while the author had made every effort to ensure the accuracy of this guidebook, changes can occur which may affect the contents. The Publishers would welcome notes of any changes you find.

Neither the author nor Questa Publishing Limited can accept responsibility for any inaccuracies, or for any injuries or damage that may occur while following the routes in this book.

Maps:

The maps accompanying the walks in this book are purely diagrammatic, and, with permission, are based on maps produced by Harvey Maps.
© Harvey Maps 2005

Published by
Questa Publishing Ltd., PO Box 520, Bamber Bridge, Preston, Lancashire PR5 8LF
and printed by
Carnmor Print, 95/97 London Road, Preston, Lancashire PR1 4BA

Contents

1
Yew Tree Tarn

This is a brief, easy and interesting walk on which to introduce young family members to country walking. Progress around the tarn is enlivened by the bright yellow expanses of marsh marigolds and flag irises along the wet ground between the tree-lined path and the water's edge. The reeds along the tarn shore provide excellent cover for coots, moorhen and mallard, while visitors early in the day may be rewarded with a glimpse of the families of greylag geese that frequent this tiny tarn. If you choose a spring day and an early start you are sure to see Yew Tree Tarn at its best.

Start: Lay-by on A593. GR322003

Total distance: 1km (½ mile)

Height gain: 10m (30 feet)

Difficulty: Easy walking on well-defined path, but with a few unguarded bridges.

1 Leave the lay-by at the southern (Coniston) end on a path that takes you to a dam at the outflow of the tarn. Cross the dam and a wooden bridge over the sluice, and then a simple, unguarded bridge. Continue for 200m/yds before crossing a small stream.

2 Follow the path through trees to a gate, shortly after which another stream is crossed by a bridge.

3 To avoid wet ground, now turn left and follow the stream to a wall junction, and here turn right and head for a wooden bridge (not immediately visible) on a grassy path through larch trees.

4 Cross the bridge, and walk along the ensuing farm track to a field gate in a wall. Don't go through the gate, but turn right alongside the wall and cross a wire fence via a gate. If you now follow the wall, it will lead you via a gate back to the lay-by at which you started.

Along the way

Yew Tree Tarn During the 19th century, James Marshall of Monk Coniston built a dam at the southern end of a former moss to create Yew Tree Tarn.

To the northern end a large rectangle with a water feed from the beck was constructed for fish breeding, and to keep the tarn stocked.

Against a backdrop of plantations of larch and oak, this artificial tarn now blends well with its surroundings. The National Trust purchased the tarn from the Marshall family in 1952.

During the late 1990s and early 2000s the National Trust has carried major repairs to the dam and the footpath around the tarn.

Yellow Flag Iris The lovely spread of yellow flag iris are a common site throughout the Lake District during spring and summer. The word *iris* is Greek for 'rainbow', though here you only find the yellow variety. The plant was a source of inspiration to English poets like Gerard Manley Hopkins, who wrote of 'Camps of yellow flag flowers blowing in the wind'. In the 12th century, the iris was adopted by the French king Louis VII in the *fleur-de-lys*, which he wore in his crusade against the Saracens.

Juniper Scrub

Locally known as 'savin' thickets of juniper are a characteristic Lakeland vegetation type, both on the uplands and the lower fells. The high-level scrub is thought to exist on the sites of former forests.

Juniper does not tolerate shading by trees, so where oaks and birches have grown to maturity, you find that the juniper has become moribund. An example of this can be seen in the woodland not far from Yew Tree Tarn, on the south side of Oxenfell, east of theConiston-Ambleside road.

2
Tarn Hows and Tarn Hows Cottage

Tarn Hows, one time water and power supply to a saw mill, was landscaped and planted by James Marshall of Monk Coniston, creating a picturesque foreground to views of the Helvellyn range and the Langdale Pikes. This walk from the head of Coniston Water passes through delightful woodland planted with large pines from North America, and returns by way of Tarn Hows Cottager, pleasantly enclosed by larch trees, and along an old pony track once used to carry slate and copper ore from Tilberthwaite to Kirby Quay on Coniston Water.

Start: Water Head car park. GR312978

Total distance: 8km (5 miles)

Height gain: 280m (920 feet)

Difficulty: This is an agreeable and quiet walk on well-maintained paths and tracks, along which the route-finding is easy.

1 From the car park take the road left along the head of the lake to a road junction. Cross-the road to a gap through which you turn right (northeast) along a fenced path beside the road, to rejoin the road at Boon Crag Cottage. (Access to the road is via an ungated gap and care should be taken for traffic).

2 Turn left in front of the cottage, cross the road, and pass in front of the next cottage to an ungated path on your left, then through a gate to a fenced path. Keep with the path to the gate onto the road.

3 Cross the road to a bridleway (signposted: Tarn Hows), and follow this as it climbs steadily through pine trees.

4 The track passes a series of pools well stocked with yellow iris, and continues through a gap in a wall – to your right a small dam creates a long narrow pool favoured by dragon- and damsel-flies. Soon the track levels, and you cross a beck, continuing past diverging tracks, right ands left, to reach a fork. Here, branch right on an ascending track (signposted:

Tarn Hows old car park) that soon narrows and climbs beside a wall. Shortly, turn left on a broad track and follow the wall to a road.

5 Cross the road, pass through an area set aside for disabled parking to reach a broad track descending northeast to wards Tarn Hows. At a cross track, turn right onto a broad well-made track (signposted; Circular

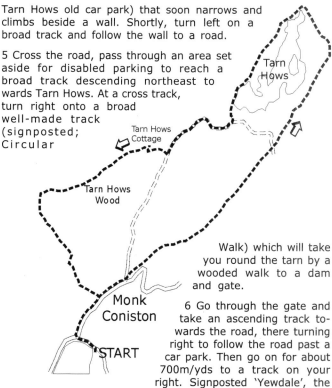

Tarn Hows

Tarn Hows Cottage

Tarn Hows Wood

Monk Coniston

START

Walk) which will take you round the tarn by a wooded walk to a dam and gate.

6 Go through the gate and take an ascending track towards the road, there turning right to follow the road past a car park. Then go on for about 700m/yds to a track on your right. Signposted 'Yewdale', the track runs between a wall on the left and mature oak and rowan trees to the right before reaching a gate into the grounds of Tarn Hows Cottage.

7 A signpost directs you left to Low Yewdale and Coniston along a path through two gates, after which you turn right on a broad, descending path, keeping ahead through trees to the banks of Yewdale Beck.

8 Turn left alongside the beck, cross a fence by a stile, and keep a hedge on your right as you make for a gate and bridge near a large tree.

9 Do not cross the beck, but go through a gate and turn left on a track, first beside the beck and then climbing between walls and fences before descending to Boon Crag Farm.

10 Stay on the track through the farm buildings and continue to the road ahead. Turn right, pass Boon Crag Cottage once more to a footpath beside the road. Use the footpath to the first gap on the left, at a road junction, where you leave the path and cross to the road opposite, following this back to the car park at Water Head.

Along the way

Tarn Hows Tarn Hows is not the name of the tarn at all. strictly, the tarn has no name, being no more than an artificial pond created by damming a stream and a few pools of marshland. The name applies not to the tarn, but to the hill above it, it is not, as is usually supposed, the 'tarn beside the hill', but the 'hill beside the tarn'.

Tarn Hows is now in the care of the National Trust, founded in 1895 by the crusading work of Canon Rawnsley, vicar of Wray and of Crosthwaite, near Keswick. In the early days, Rawnsley's chief concern was the threat to the Lake District posed by the developers of housing estates and railway.

Tarn Hows was bought by Beatrix Potter, better known locally as Mrs William Heelis. She sold half at cost to the Trust (the purchase being funded by Sir Samuel Scott), and bequeathed the other half.

The Trust has created a new section of path around the tarns to enable those with walking difficulties to enjoy the place, but there are unavoidably some steep inclines that could cause problems for visitors in wheelchairs without the company of some strong helpers.

Boon Crag farm and cottage Formerly part of the Monk Coniston Estate, and purchased by Beatrix Potter in 1930, the farm is still active, while the cottage and its outbuildings are a maintenance depot for the work of the National Trust.

3
Tom Heights and Hodge Close

This outstanding walk starts by ascending through peaceful oak woodland, along the course of Tom Gill with its cascading beck and attractive waterfalls, and leads to Tarn Hows. With only a brief halt at this popular spot, the walk goes on to explore the volcanic outcrops that adorn tom Heights, which provide remarkable views of Coniston Water and the broad sweep of the Lakeland fells from the Old Man of Coniston to the long, undulating line of the Helvellyn and Fairfield massifs. Hodge Close is renowned for the high quality of its green-hued slate, which it supplied to the world.

Start: Glen Mary Bridge. GR322999

Total distance: 8km (5 miles)

Height gain: 360m (1180 feet)

Difficulty: Pleasant walking through wooded glens, along narrow country lanes and across the craggy undulating top of Tom Heights

The path down into Hodge Close Quarry has in the past few years been subject to many rock falls and it is no longer safe to descend to view the quarry at close quarters.

Children will need careful supervision in the vicinity of Hodge Close, where the quarry waters are over 30m (100ft) deep, and have very steep sides.

1 From the parking area cross Tom Gill by a wooden bridge and ascend its left (true right) bank, passing cascades and a delightful waterfall, to reach the dam of Tarn Hows.

2 Turn left along a well-made track circling the tarn. Shortly after you pass a wire fence on your right, go left on a path climbing through rowan and silver birch and across bracken-clad slopes to reach the rocky crest of Tom Heights, with its magnificent views, at a small cairn.

3 Continue along the undulating crest of the fell passing two

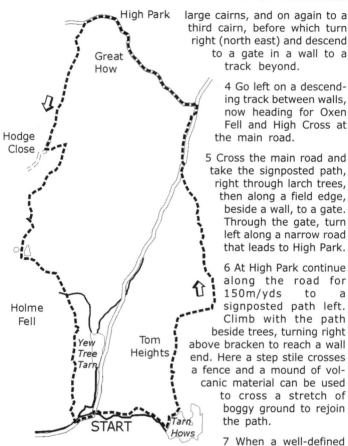

large cairns, and on again to a third cairn, before which turn right (north east) and descend to a gate in a wall to a track beyond.

4 Go left on a descending track between walls, now heading for Oxen Fell and High Cross at the main road.

5 Cross the main road and take the signposted path, right through larch trees, then along a field edge, beside a wall, to a gate. Through the gate, turn left along a narrow road that leads to High Park.

6 At High Park continue along the road for 150m/yds to a signposted path left. Climb with the path beside trees, turning right above bracken to reach a wall end. Here a step stile crosses a fence and a mound of volcanic material can be used to cross a stretch of boggy ground to rejoin the path.

7 When a well-defined path branches left, follow it (after prolonged rain this section can be very wet) and head for a gate and track into woodland, on the way passing a long-forgotten bracken cutter. In the woodland, follow the track to a group of houses, Hodge Close. Pass the first house on your right, then through a gate bear left on a rising ground a garage to.

8 From the garage, take the gated track on the left to pass a reed-filled dam, continue to a gate on your right, signposted 'Yewdale'. Go through the gate and follow a track with a fence

10

to the right. Descend to another gate, but don't go through this one.

9 Turn left on an ascending track to yet another gate. You can go through this one, after which, at the top of the climb, take the track running back, left, into a quarry.

10 From the quarry, take the second path on your right, ascending to a small disused reservoir, and here bear right, crossing the dam, and follow the water's edge to a boggy gully opposite the dam.

11 Keep as much as possible to dry ground, and turn right (south-southeast) alongside the gully, and aim for a col on the skyline. When you reach it, cross the collapsed wall, and begin descending on a stony path, passing a large boulder to a large cairn.

12 From the cairn, white arrows way mark the route, via gates to Yew Tree Farm, with its fine-spinning gallery, used for the drying of wool and yarn.

13 Go past the farm to the road, and there cross the road to a gate. Through the gate, turn left, and go along the field edge to a gate giving into the car park.

Along the way

Monk Coniston Estate Formerly owned by James Marshal, a noted geologist who studied the metamorphic rocks of the area. The Marshals were responsible for damming many small tarns on the estate to provide fishing for guests. The estate was purchased in 1930 by Beatrix Potter, and is now in the ownership of the National Trust.

Hodge Close Quarry Many of the small quarries to be seen in the Lakeland fells were to supply stone for local wall building. Most builders recycled stone, which was a fifth of the price of new stone, but as building increased so the demand for stone and roofing slate grew. Hodge Close supplied both to the local trade and much further afield.

Today the quarry is a playground for rock climbers, and the deep waters entertain sub aqua divers who explore the many side tunnels. What is especially pleasing, however, is to see the way nature has started to recolonise the workings with oak, birch and hazel.

11

4
Old Man of Coniston

Until twenty or so years ago, the Old Man of Coniston was the highest summit in Lancashire, then it was transferred, with a great swathe of Lancashire-over –the-Sands, to Cumbria. The distinction brought many walkers to its summit, but the dictates of bureaucracy have scarcely lessened the attraction this distinguished summit receives. Today, this the most southerly of the high Lakeland fells, still attracts walkers every day of the year.

The following walk briefly visits old quarry workings which extracted a most beautiful green slate from the mountain for more than three centuries, before calling at a high mountain tarn set in a steep-sided cradle directly beneath the summit.

Start: Disused quarry, Walna Scar Road. GR289970

Total distance: 7.5km (4¾ miles)

Height gain: 590m (1935 feet)

Difficulty: A rewarding walk that will be a good test of most children's temperament and determination.

Not to be tackled in poor visibility. The summit is very close to the edge of a steep drop.

Young children will find the final, steep section strenuous. If in doubt, the best approach is to plan only to go as far as Low Water, to have a good rest while watching others toil up the slopes, and then decide whether to try them yourself.

The start of the walk is reached by a climbing drive from Coniston, by a narrow road behind the railway station. When this road passes through an intake gate to open fell you will find the quarry parking space a short distance ahead, on the left.

1 Leave the parking area and head back towards the gate, there turning left to walk easily along a broad track (signposted: Coniston Old Man, Low Water). The track starts alongside a wall, which quickly falls away to the right, while the track climbs gradually for almost a mile to a sharp left turn at the back of a rocky mound. Ignore any paths on the right, but follow the main trail as it climbs roughly, twisting about as it meets the first of many slate spoil heaps.

2 The spoil heaps are not an attractive sight, but they remain an important part of our industrial heritage. It would be nice if someone put all the slack back where it came from; meanwhile we must accept it for what it is, industrial archaeology.

3 The upward path is never in doubt. Across the base of spoil heaps, it becomes loose under foot, and slippery in wet conditions. As you climb beside a slate wall you pass beneath steel hawsers that where used to convey slate to the valley. Soon, at a bend, you encounter the remains of quarry sheds that are worth a moment's investigation, but do resist the temptation to explore any mining levels you find burrowing into the hillside, they are now all dangerous.

4 Continue ever upwards, passing more cables, just before your third encounter with these rusting remnants you can take a path, right, climbing to a narrow col, beyond which lies Low Water.

A word of warning is needed! Do not go beneath the third set of cables. A large cave-like quarry lies beyond, but this has seen many roof-falls in recent years and is now most unstable and unsafe. Make sure young children do not run on ahead.

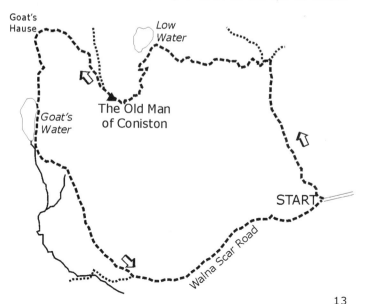

13

5 When you reach Low Water you can cross the outflow and find a comfortable spot on the opposite bank from which to assess your enthusiasm for the steep pull to the summit which lies beyond.

6 Returning to the main path, follow it upwards in zigzags. The last section is a little loose and eroded, but will not cause problems for carefully-placed feet. On reaching more level ground, a broad path climbs less steeply to the summit plateau, crowned by a large cairn on a plinth, and a trig pillar very close to the edge of the corrie housing Low Water. Keep children under close supervision at this point.

7 A simple retracing of steps, taking care on the descent to Low Water, is the quickest way back.

8 For a longer circuit, and a splendid way of concluding the walk leave the summit, keeping the corrie on your right, but keep a look out for a cairn at the start of a path left. (Do not take the first uncairned path in a shallow dip, this only leads to the top of a crag and problems). This leads down a rocky pathway to reach a high mountain pass, Goat's Hawse, rather a wet place to be.

9 Before getting embroiled in bogginess, go left, down a good, but loose, path to reach the end of Goat's water, a magnificent mountain lake set most dramatically beneath the towering cliffs of Dow Crag.

10 Follow the path through the boulders at the water's edge, gradually leaving the lake behind to cross a low rocky rib that has a moment or two of downward squirming (all avoidable) before following an easy course to a large cairn at its junction with the Walna Scar Road. Turn left, and follow the road (a motorable highway, though not a recommended one) back to the starting point, passing diminutive, reed-filled Boo Tarn on the way.

Along the way

Slate quarries Slate has been quarried from Old Man for over three centuries, yielding large quantities of high quality green slate which was in demand all around the world as building material. The walk passes the remains of dressing sheds and winch wheel housings, and there are many tunnels used by the miners. Many of these have wooden floors covered with rubble, and most are now rotten; a fall of some hundreds of feet awaits the incautious.

5
Wetherlam from Tilberthwaite

This fine, but energetic, ascent of Wetherlam from Tilberthwaite is a popular walk and well within the capabilities of most children, though some previous upland experience would be an advantage.

Tilberthwaite Gill is a chasm of great natural beauty, a deep gash in the landscape hidden among the hills and unseen from the roadway. It is a spot that was tremendously popular with Victorian visitors who linked precarious footpaths and rickety wooden bridges to view the spectacle.

The featureless top of Wetherlam makes this an inappropriate walk in poor visibility.

Start: Car park, Tilberthwaite. GR306010

Total distance: 7.5km (4½ miles)

Difficulty: Most of the walk is on well-made miners' tracks, finishing by a rocky pull to the summit. The return is by a grassy plateau and green path beside Crook Beck.

The height gain may prove too much for very young children (and a few adults!) though this is a fine outing on which to introduce children to sustained uphill work. Well-timed words of encouragement will work wonders.

1 Leave the car park by the steps to gain a signposted footpath ascending quarry spoil to a path junction beside a hut ruin. Near the ruin, the second entrance on your left gives a view into Penny Rigg Quarry, its vertical edge much favoured by rock climbers, but no place for young children.

2 Take the right hand path which sets off level, then descend by steps to a bridge over the bubbling waters of Tilberthwaite Gill.

3 Cross the bridge to a stepped path to climb out of the gill, through a gate and continue climbing to a path junction. Take the left fork through bracken to join a miner's track.

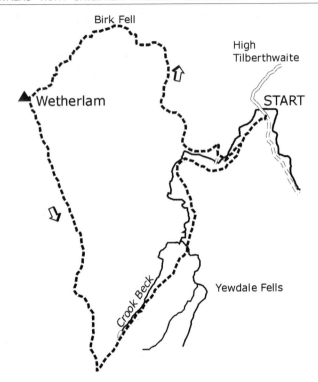

4 Here turn left, with the track running close by the ravine in which cascading water can be heard but is obscured from view by trees. At a junction bear right, keeping to the main path to reach a small side stream.

5 As you step over the stream note to your left the ruins of the old Tilberthwaite Mine and its yellow-brown copper spoil tips. This mine is especially dangerous, some of the shafts being over 500 feet deep.

6 Continue along the track as it climbs gently to more waste tips and ruined cabins at Hellen's Mine. From here the track skirts the wet basin of the wettest Dry Cove in Lakeland to reach Borlase Mine.

7 From the mine take a stepped path ascending, right, in

zigzags between rock outcrops to Birk Fell Hawes, a narrow col between Birk Fell and Wetherlam.

8 Once you reach the Hawes, and after a moment's rest (well-earned) set of southwest for a delightful and easy scramble up Wetherlam Edge to the summit of Wetherlam.

9 Leave the fell top in a roughly south-easterly direction, crossing the grassy plateau to a large cairn, that marks the start of a distinct cairned path descending for some distance to a small tarn at the top of Hole Rake Pass.

10 At the tarn turn left (northeast) on a grassy track, continue past a quarry entrance, and descend alongside Crook Beck, which is contained in a pleasant gill.

11 Step over a small beck above a rowan-lined waterfall, and keep with the cairned path to a large cairn at a stream crossing. Here turn right on a path to circle above the slopes of Tilberthwaite Gill.

12 Pass a small cairn on a waste heap, to reach a rocky step across a small side stream. Press on to the hut ruin encountered at the start of the walk, and from there retrace your steps to the car park.

Slate quarrying

Though lacking the glamour of mineral mines, slate quarrying has played an immensely important part in the economy of the Lake District. Even so, it is a robber industry in the sense that you cannot replace what is taken away, and great spoil heaps are left to mar the landscape for all eternity.

Two of the underlying rocks of the Lake District produce marketable slates - the Borrowdale Volcanic Series, and the Silurian Beds. Ironically, the oldest rocks, the Skiddaw Slates, only produce slates of poor, unworkable quality.

The colour of the slates varies: the lovely soft greens come from the volcanic beds, while those of Silurian origin tend to be mainly blue or a drab grey.

6
Greenburn Copper Mine and the Cathedral

The wild and isolated valley of Greenburn, once home to one of Lakeland's major copper mines and a place of much industry and business, is now quiet and seldom-visited.

The stream bank between the mine workings and the dammed tarn has many pleasant picnic sites and small rock pools, though care needs to be exercised in the vicinity of the mines, where there are many open shafts.

There is much of fascination here, but all children must be closely supervised and kept well away from mine shafts and inviting pools of water.

Start: Tilberthwaite car park. GR306010

Total distance: 8km (5 miles)

Height gain: 590m (1935 feet)

Difficulty: A pleasant walk using old mine tracks and steep fellside paths. The visit to Cathedral quarry entails the use stepping stone along a short wet tunnel. There is always an element of risk in the vicinity of any Lakeland quarry or mine, and Greenburn is no exception.

Young children must be closely supervised.

1 Leave Tilberthwaite car park by the steps, and follow the directions given in Walk 5 as far as Hellen's Mine.

2 At Hellen's Mine, turn right (northeast), passing old cabins and a partially blocked shaft, to a col boasting a stand of windswept Scots pines that are reason enough for a moment's pause.

3 Descend from the col among tree stumps to a tree-lined hollow containing a small bog. Turn left, keeping the bog and a fence on your left, and continue, ignoring two stiles, descending alongside the fence as it turns right (east) to wards a wall junction.

4 Cross the fence by a stile about 100m/yds before the wall, and head (northwards) towards a grassy mound close by the wall. Now follow the wall (northeast) descending past a stile to a track in the valley bottom. An expanse of ground just before the track is very wet, but can be avoided on the left, joining the track 100m/yds from a gate. Once on the track, turn left (west) and follow it to the remains of Greenburn Mine.

5 If you bear left at a junction before the mine, you can walk among the ruined mine buildings. If you go right, you cross a stream flowing from the mine ruins to follow a path beside Greenburn Beck to the dam of Greenburn Reservoir. The grassy stream banks are an ideal place for lunch.

6 Return to the main track and head (east) out of the valley. At the gate, cross the stile and continue on the track to a junction.

7 Bear right and go past the next turning on the right,

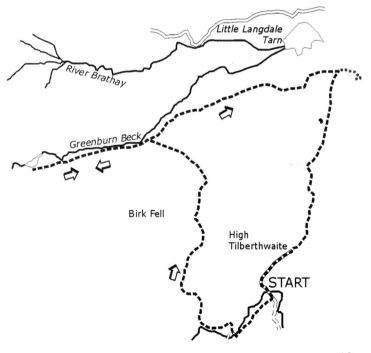

continuing to a gate and walled track. Through the gate, follow the track past two cottages, High and Low Garth, to a wooden gate. Go through the gate for 100m/yds to a rising track and gate on the right. Take this track to a flat area where, on your right, you find the dark entrance to a tunnel. Go through the tunnel using stepping-stones to reach the large amphitheatre of Cathedral Quarry.

DO NOT GO PAST THE CENTRAL PILLAR, THERE IS A VERY DEEP WATER-FILLED SHAFT BEYOND.

DO NOT CLIMB ON THE BOULDERS, THEY ARE UNSAFE.

8 Return to the tunnel entrance and take the descending track on the left to return to the gate on the main track.

9 Go through the gate and after about 75m/yds, take a quarry track on your left. At a flat area turn left to a gate and footpath sign. Follow the path, climbing a steep meadow to cross the top wall by a step and gap stile.

10 Keeping a wall on your left continue (south) up the fell to ruined huts, and here bear right (southwest) to pick up a track near a gate. Turn left (south) to pass through the gate and press on along the track to High Tilberthwaite Farm, followed by a short stretch of road walking to reach the car park.

Along the way

Greenburn Mine The mine extracted copper from seven veins, with the greatest period of prosperity coming between 1854 and 1861, when more than a thousand tons of ore were extracted. The seven mile journey to the rail head at Coniston ultimately made the mine uneconomic.

Among the ruined buildings it is still possible to identify the dressing floors and two water wheels. The reservoir dam was breached by the same heavy storm which in 1966 destroyed Stockley Bridge in upper Borrowdale. Here it caused severe damage to the mine site and to farms downstream.

The Cathedral This large cavern was worked by quarrymen known locally as "Old Men", who would have worked by candlelight on wooden platforms, nerve able to see as a whole the vast cathedral-like cavern with its central pillar they had created. The hole now allowing in light was made by later workings above, while the water beyond fills a deep shaft to lower levels.

7
Tarn Hows via Tom Gill

The Tarns, or Tarn Hows, must be one of the most beautiful and much-visited places in southern Lakeland. The most common approach, by car from Hawkshead, poses problems along the narrow lanes. By contrast, this walk from the main Coniston to Ambleside road has no such difficulties, and ascends through the wooded ravine of Tom Gill with its waterfalls and rocky cascades. The first glimpse of the tarn as your head rises above the small dam will linger in your memory for years to come, and encourage many revisits.

Start: Glen Mary Bridge. GR322999

Total distance: 4km (2½ miles)

Height gain: 150m (490 feet)

Difficulty: An easy walk, ideal for children who have not done much walking. The ascent, on a rough and stony path, crosses a few unbridged streams, but the walk around the tarn is on a well-maintained path, constructed with handicapped visitors in mind.

1 Leave the parking area by crossing the wooden bridge spanning Tom Gill. Turn right through a gate on a terraced path to follow the Gill upstream. When you come level with the waterfalls take the lower path for a closer look at the falls. From here, a well-made path continues through a gate then by crossing a rocky outcrop to a small moss-covered dam and the tarn outflow.

2 At no point during this ascent should you cross the stream; there are no stiles over the wall or fence higher up to enable you to get back.

3 Above the dam turn left on a well-maintained path that forms part of the Cumbria Way. Keep with the main track (waymarked) at any turning on the left. Go through a gate and follow a barbed wire fence to a wooden bridge, after which the track ascends to a junction. Continue ahead (waymarked).

4 The way now crosses open ground with views over the tarn, and numerous pleasant picnic spots away from the crowds that gather around the car parks.

5 At another gate continue with the track until, after passing a stand of pine trees on your right, you can turn right on a path crossing grassy slopes above the tarn to bring you on to a track leading back to the outflow.

6 Turning left, away from the tarn, ascend the track for 50 m/yds to a signposted 'Wheelchair' path to the right. Take the

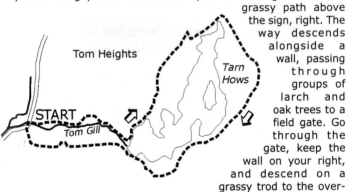

grassy path above the sign, right. The way descends alongside a wall, passing through groups of larch and oak trees to a field gate. Go through the gate, keep the wall on your right, and descend on a grassy trod to the over-grown remains of Lane Head Farm. Turn sharp right and cross a field to another gate, beyond which a stony lane will lead you back to the start.

Along the way

Tom Gill This little oak-lined ravine with a small waterfall, cascades and rock pools carries the outflow from the tarns, and was renamed by John Ruskin, who lived nearby at Brantwood. Not satisfied with the name, Tom Gill for such a beautiful spot, Ruskin renamed it 'Glen Mary', which touched a note of accord with the public, and explains the name of the 'Glen Mary Bridge' on the main road.

Bracken harvest

Until recent times, bracken was harvested for use as animal bedding, thatching and making potash. Much of the machinery used for the harvest is still to be found on the fells, only to be reclaimed when a tenant farmer sells up and needs to recover his money.

8
White Maiden
from Torver

White Maiden and nearby White Pike are seldom visited by walkers, so this walk provides an opportunity to wander across trackless fells, and to practice navigation techniques.

The view from White Maiden is extensive and embraces the dark form of Black Combe, the silver sands of the Duddon estuary, Scafell Pike, and on a clear day, Ingleborough in the Yorkshire Dales.

Start: Lay-by on the A593, near track junction. GR285945

Total distance: 10.5km (6½ miles)

Height gain: 540m (1770 feet)

Difficulty: Moderate; the walk uses stone tracks and good paths to the top of Walna Scar Pass, and then crosses open country without clear pathways. As a result the walk is not recommended on days of poor visibility.

1 Leave the lay-by parking area by a tarmac track signposted for Coniston Old Man and Walna Scar. The track is waymarked through the village of Scar Head and leads to a walled bridleway.

2 Follow the bridleway through two gates and past a stone barn to a third gate. Go through this gate also and on over a bridge spanning Tanearth Beck, then keep ahead on a rough track to gated sheep pens, follow blue arrow markers through the pens. Turn sharp right to a wooden bridge over Torver Beck.

3 Once over the beck, turn left to pass between quarry waste heaps and climb beside a tree-lined gully. Care is needed just here because the gully is the entrance to a quarry and has steep and loose sides.

4 Climb to a wire fence, turn right to circle around the edge of Bannishead Quarry. Of the grass paths that then appear ahead, take that on the left and climb easily to Walna Scar Road. (Ignore the prominent large cairn, which marks the start of a path to Goat's Water).

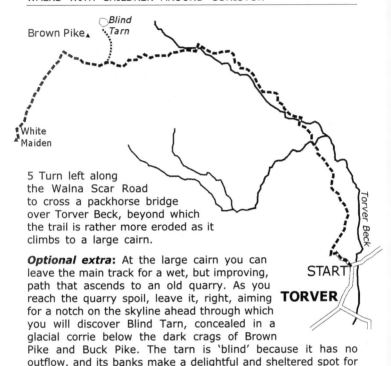

5 Turn left along the Walna Scar Road to cross a packhorse bridge over Torver Beck, beyond which the trail is rather more eroded as it climbs to a large cairn.

Optional extra: At the large cairn you can leave the main track for a wet, but improving, path that ascends to an old quarry. As you reach the quarry spoil, leave it, right, aiming for a notch on the skyline ahead through which you will discover Blind Tarn, concealed in a glacial corrie below the dark crags of Brown Pike and Buck Pike. The tarn is 'blind' because it has no outflow, and its banks make a delightful and sheltered spot for lunch. *To continue...*return to the main track...

6 Follow the Walna Scar track past a number of small cairns and a small stone shelter on the right – a couple of very close friends might just squeeze in there in an emergency!

7 A small cairn to the right of the path marks the top of the pass, so here, turn left to climb the grassy fellside (on path) to a cairn marking the summit of a grassy ridge, Walna Scar. Continue southwest a path dose now lead you to a shallow col from which you leave the path left and climb another grassy slope to the unexpectedly rocky summit of White Maiden, its cairn close by the angle of a wall, and overlooking the sweeping expanse of Torver High Common.

8 To return, simply retrace your steps, no less an enjoyable experience for treading familiar ground. In the lee of Walna Scar, on perfect days, you can wile away much time comfortably resting against a boulder, listening to the sound of silence.

9
Monk Coniston Moor

The oak forest of Monk Coniston Moor was coppiced during the sixteenth and seventeenth centuries to produce charcoal which was then used in bloomeries where ore was smelted, or for the making gunpowder.

These delightful woodlands have now been absorbed by the Forestry Commission into the Forest of Grisedale, and this walk takes you along quiet tracks, away from the main visitor areas, and affords splendid views across Coniston Water.

Start: Water Head car park. GR316978
Total distance: 9.5km (6 miles)
Height gain: 270m (885 feet)
Difficulty: Easy walking along forest trails, wet in places. Care is needed on the final busy road section

1 At the car park entrance turn right along the road a short distance to as right-hand bend. Cross the road to a signposted footpath, and follow a fence-lined path (east).

2 At the end of the path, go through the gate and turn left to follow a well-signposted footpath diversion, first around the edge of a field, then through the garden of Rowlinson Ground. The diversion ends down steps to the house access drive, there turn left.

3 Follow the signs for Hawkshead, and through the drive gates turn left onto the road, shortly passing an old slate fence to reach a track on the right.

4 Turn right (south) along the track and go through a gate onto a forest trail. Walk along the trail, taking the left branch at the first junction. Keep to the main trail when a grass track leaves on the left, and continue to the next cross-roads, here turn left.

5 Follow the trail to the left as it climbs in zigzags past wind-damaged trees (tarn below to the left) to a T-junction. Turn left and follow the trail to a clearing on the left. After 75m/yds, take a turning back to the right on an ascending track, and follow

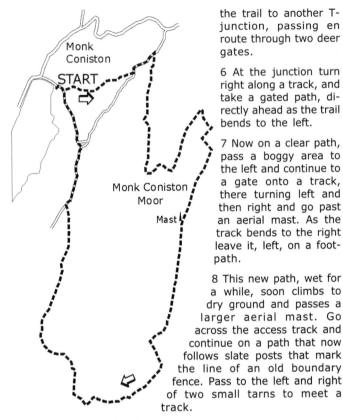

the trail to another T-junction, passing en route through two deer gates.

6 At the junction turn right along a track, and take a gated path, directly ahead as the trail bends to the left.

7 Now on a clear path, pass a boggy area to the left and continue to a gate onto a track, there turning left and then right and go past an aerial mast. As the track bends to the right leave it, left, on a footpath.

8 This new path, wet for a while, soon climbs to dry ground and passes a larger aerial mast. Go across the access track and continue on a path that now follows slate posts that mark the line of an old boundary fence. Pass to the left and right of two small tarns to meet a track.

9 Turn left, passing two tracks to the left, rising gently to the brow of a hill, and then descending right, through trees on a rough path (signposted Bridleway) to the buildings at Lawson Park.

10 Cross the access track to a path (yellow waymarker), and follow a descending track through a gate, accompanying a stonewall to a bridge and past a barn.

11 Pleasant birch woodland ensues, through which the trail continues to a gate at the road.

12 Turn right along the road, taking care not to tangle with traffic on this busy back road, until you return to the car park.

10
Coniston Bloomery

Encouraged by the monks of Furness Abbey, the woodlands of south Lakeland were burned for charcoal to be used in bloomeries for the smelting of iron ore, most notably from medieval times until the 17th century.

This pleasant walk visits Coniston Hall, the oldest building in Coniston, and then meanders along the wooded shore of Coniston Water to the site of a bloomery that flourished here 400 years or so ago. The walk returns to Coniston along the trackbed of the disused Furness Railway.

Start: Coniston main car park. GR303976

Total distance: 9km (5½ miles)

Height gain: 110m (360 feet)

Difficulty: An easy walk along well-signposted paths and tracks, with only a few unbridged streams to negotiate.

1 Leave the car park, turning left in front of the church to the bridge spanning Church Beck. Cross the bridge, go left, past the petrol station, to the next turning on the left (signposted: Gondola).

2 Turn left here and follow the road for 400m/yds until the road turns sharp left. At this point cross the road to a gate and a signposted footpath. Turn right along a pathway beside a hedge, to a gate. Now, with a fence on your left, the path takes you to a broad track heading for Coniston Hall.

3 In the grounds of Coniston Hall, follow signposts, right then left, to a campsite, and when in the camp field. Keep with the road to a waymarked track to the left. This will take you down to the lakeshore and a small gate in a wall.

4 From the wall, the lush green field you see in front of you is the site of the Coniston Bloomery, and was once covered with ash and waste heaps from the smelting process.

5 Stay along the lakeshore, heading for a gate leading into another campsite, past the finger post and stay with the shore (waymarked) passing a slipway to a track leading into Torver

Common Wood. Use the broad track into the woodland, staying close by the lake until a sign directs you left crossing a small stream on a path to a clearing and a sign for Torver.

CONISTON

START

6 To return, turn right (west), and on a broad path cross a vehicle track and go though a collapsed wall, after which the path is enclosed by trees and climbs to a gate and signpost (Torver Commons).

Haws Bank

7 Go through the gate on to a track leading to a gate beside a barn. Beyond the gate, follow an enclosed track leading to another gate. Through the gate, turn right, through another gate, and then by a hawthorn-lined green path cross four gated fields. In the fifth field head for a gate in the wall directly opposite. Beyond the gate, take a clear path for 100m/yds through a conifer plantation to a field. Through this gate go right along the edge of the woodland to the rear of Hoathwaite Farm.

Coniston Hall Park

Bloomery (site of)

Coniston Water

Hoathwaite Farm

8 The on-going path takes you through gated sheep pens to the farmyard. Turn left out of the farm and at the entrance take the gate on your right into a camping field.

9 Cross the top of the field with the fence on your left, and go past a cattle grid until you reach a grass track descending to a beck and gate into a larch woodland. Stay with the track beside the beck to as ladder stile, and go over the stile to cross the beck by a bridge.

10 The way now follows a grass track, at times indistinctly, but setting off ahead, then bearing left to follow the base of rising ground (do not head for the caravans that can be seen through trees to the right) to a gate in a wall. The gate gives access to the old Furness railway track, and once through it turn right

(signposted: Coniston) to follow way marking past the caravan site entrance, then by a grassy track to a gate beside a seat. The gate leads to the main road. Follow this for 100m/yds until the road bends sharply to the right. The onward route is the signposted track on the left, leading back on to the course of the old railway.

11 The trackbed is now followed back to Coniston, its tree-lined course giving splendid views of Coniston Water and the tree-cloaked hills beyond. Shortly after passing under an arched slate bridge you arrive at a new housing estate on the site of Coniston station. Follow the on-going path to join a road past small workshops and the mountain rescue post to a junction.

12 Turn right on a descending road past the Sun Hotel to the Church Beck bridge. Cross the beck by the footbridge and go past the church to return to the car park.

Along the way

Coniston Hall This charming building was built in the 15th century by the Flemings, and there is evidence of an earlier hall on the site.

Certainly, W G Collingwood comments that Coniston Hall was 'the seat of the Flemings from about 1250 to some time after 1700', the family having gained Coniston in 1250 by marriage, making it their principle seat for seven generations.

Sir Daniel Fleming was born of the Coniston family in 1633. He went to Queen's College, Oxford, and to Guy's Inn, and followed his father in the cause of King Charles, losing much in pocket and his prospects. So he left Coniston Hall and moved to Rydal, which had been the Fleming's second home since about 1484.

Bloomeries So important was the charcoal available from the Furness woods that many bloomery sites are found near to the timber source rather than the iron mine.

The iron probably came up the lake or on packhorse to the smithies which were also located near fast-flowing streams which provided the water power.

11
Dow Crag
and Goat's Water

This is a pleasant but challenging walk making use of old quarry tracks to gain height to the top of Walna Scar, a high mountain pass linking Coniston with Dunnerdale. The way continues along a fine rocky ridge to the top of Dow Crag overlooking Goat's Water, by way of which the walk concludes.

This is an outstanding excursion for youngsters, a full mountaineering walk, and sure to give them immense satisfaction, but it may be beyond very young children.

Start: Lay-by on the A593, near track junction. GR285945

Total distance: 11km (7 miles)

Height gain: 670m (2195 feet)

Difficulty: Demanding, and with considerable height gain, but an excellent introduction to high fell walking. A fine clear day is required.

1 Leave the lay-by along the tarmac track signposted to Coniston Old Man and Walna Scar. Follow the waymarking through the village of Scar Head to join a walled bridleway. Walk on, to the third gate spanning the track, and there go through a gate to cross a bridge spanning Tranearth Beck, then by a rough track to gated sheep pens. Blue waymarking now directs you to a wooden bridge over Torver Beck. Once across the bridge turn left to pass between quarry waste heaps, then climb beside a tree-lined gully, the entrance to quarry workings, and dangerous.

2 Climb to a wire fence, turn right to circle the edge of the quarry, and on the opposite side take a terraced path left, climbing to the Walna Scar road. Turn left to cross a packhorse bridge over Torver Beck. Once across the bridge the track becomes more eroded as it climbs to a large cairn.

3 Continue, ascending all the while, passing small cairns and a small stone shelter on the right.

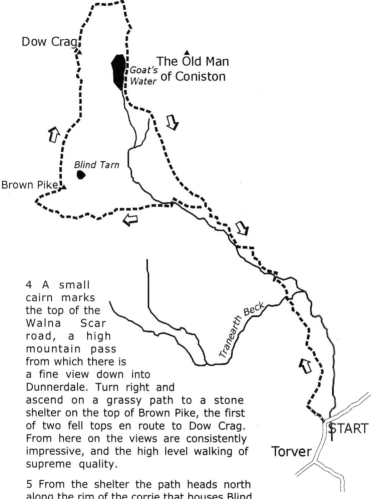

4 A small cairn marks the top of the Walna Scar road, a high mountain pass from which there is a fine view down into Dunnerdale. Turn right and ascend on a grassy path to a stone shelter on the top of Brown Pike, the first of two fell tops en route to Dow Crag. From here on the views are consistently impressive, and the high level walking of supreme quality.

5 From the shelter the path heads north along the rim of the corrie that houses Blind Tarn (Walk 8 describes a route to the tarn from the Walna Scar road).

6 Press on along the ridge, crossing another minor summit, Buck Pike, on the way, and then heading for Dow Crag by a

31

stony path. As you approach Dow Crag, the immense cliffs falling to Goat's Water below become more pronounced and the path crosses the top of one or two yawning gullies; children will need close supervision here, and whilst on the fine rocky summit of Dow Crag.

7 From this point everything is downhill, but only physically. You may be leaving behind the magnificent views from the top of Dow Crag, but the return beside Goat's Water is walking of the highest order.

8 From the top of Dow Crag go north, continuing your original direction, on a clear rocky path which soon turns northeast to descend to Goat's Hawes, a boggy col linking Dow Crag and the Old Man of Coniston.

9 Go down to the Hawes and as the path starts to ascend on the other side take a path off to the right and descend to Goat's Water. The path is loose and slippery in places.

10 Use the path along the left shore of Goat's Water, passing through scattered boulders, and following a good path that leads all the way out of the valley, to a cairn on the Walna Scar road, not far from the point at which you first joined it.

11 Cross the track to a green path, and descend to the wire fencing around Bannishead Quarry, from where you retrace your steps to Torver.

Coniston Forest

When the Norse people first settled among the fells of Furness, and around the great lake which they named Thorstanes Watter, the valley and lower fells of Coniston were dense with growths of oak, holly, ash, hazel and birch.

By the 16th century all this had gone, and of the great oak woods there remained but a few scattered trees and the enormous beams in such buildings as Coniston Old Hall.

By the time of Henry VIII all the fells were bare of timber, the forests all but gone, leaving 'lytell short Okes...[but] no tymber of any valewe'.

12
Boulder Valley and Levers Water

Starting from the Walna Scar road, this pleasant walk on little-used paths threads a way through a valley of large boulders deposited by a retreating glacier at the end of the last Ice Age, about 10,000 years ago.

With many places at which to stop for lunch, the walk continues to Levers Water, and returns through Coppermines Valley, scene of much fascinating industrial activity in ages gone by.

Start: Disused quarry, Walna Scar road. GR289970

Total distance: 6km (4 miles)

Height gain: 290m (950 feet)

Difficulty: a pleasant walk using old quarry tracks and clear footpaths, but flanked by many deep mine shafts.

1 Leave the parking area on a track heading northwest alongside a wall, which falls away as the track climbs. After about a mile the track turns sharply to the left around a rocky mound. As it does, take the second path on the right, a terraced track high above Coppermines valley, which takes you on, past the entrance to an old mine.

2 As you pass the mine entrance the track ends, and you should follow a path past a large boulder, known as the Pudding Stone, to descend to a wooden bridge crossing Low Water Beck. Beyond lies Boulder Valley.

3 Cross the bridge, and follow a rocky path ascending on the right of the valley. As you climb, make for a large boulder perched on a col on the skyline. From the col, descend, passing en route a number of mines shafts enclosed by wire fences, to meet the shore path of Levers Water. Now turn right past the fenced entrance to Simon's Mine (do not cross the fence, the ground on the other side is loose and unstable, and the mine more than 450 feet deep!). Cross Lever's Water dam and a causeway to a track descending on the right.

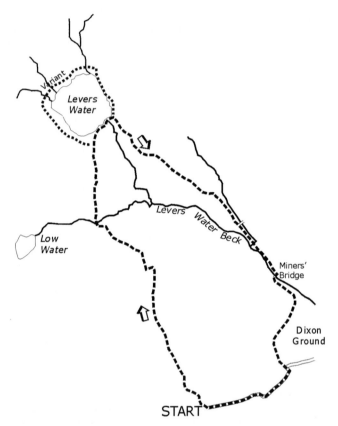

Optional extra

When you meet the shore path at Lever's Water you can turn left to follow a clear path all the way round the tarn to reach the causeway.

To return...

4 Follow the broad descending track (southeast) to a row of iron posts crossing the track. The track here swings right, but you continue ahead to a broad green path. The path descends, then turns left, with a descending path right. Take this path on the right, surmounting a small rock step and then continuing

through bracken to the rear of a slate building.

You are now in Coppermines Valley which during the 1800s was a scene of much activity, with crushing and sorting sheds, and mine offices.

Today most of these buildings have gone, but a private venture is undertaking restoration work to produce a heritage site.

5 Turn right on a track through the heritage site to a gate between two white buildings. Go through the gate and follow the track to the left, then turn right to pass a row of cottages (Irish Row) on your left. Keep with the track as it descends with a wide stream on your right. Pass the remains of a dam to a gated bridge (Miners' Bridge).

6 Cross the bridge and the track to reach a path that turns left to run behind a stone wall. Take this path as it climbs steadily, with good views over Coniston village and the lake to the fells of Monk Coniston Moor.

7 When you meet a wall, follow it to cross a bridge, and pass through two gates to a stile. Cross the stile and turn right on a tarmac road, then round a right hand bend to climb to the fell gate just before the parking area. Take care along this stretch of road, which is very narrow.

Along the way

Coppermines valley To encourage mining production, royal patronage was granted by Elizabeth 1 by the setting up in 1561 of the Society for the Mines Royal. The mines of the Coniston fells saw large-scale exploitation from 1599 onwards, the main mine lying in Church Beck, though this first start ended in 1650. In 1758 the Macclesfield Copper Company obtained the lease of the Coniston mines, worked them for a while until all the known ore bodies were worked out. In 1830, a Cornish tin miner, John Barratt, arrived with new knowledge and techniques, and quickly stepped up production. By 1849 the Coniston Mining Company employed 400 men and was removing about 250 tons of ore a month.

All was not sweetness and light, however, for in 1620 there was a complaint at Coniston concerning 'both meadowe and Cornelande as is decayed and wasted' owing to the pollution of the Church Beck 'by Reasone of the Stamphowse and braying of the Coper vre [ore] and other Rubbishe at the saide Stamphowse.'

13
Torver Back Common

An easy walk using woodland paths, lakeshore and moorland paths, that provides ample opportunity to linger by the lake or savour the views from the grassy mounds of Torver Common.

Start: Lay-by on A593, near track junction. GR285945

Total distance: 8.5 km (5¼ miles)

Height gain: 250m (820 feet)

Difficulty: Easy; a few wet stretches and unbridged streams, finishing with a short section along a narrow busy road.

1 From the lay-by walk along the road towards Coniston. Cross the bridge over Torver Beck and turn right through an iron wicket gate into a field. Go along the edge of the field, with a fence on your left, past a gate, to a gap-stile and boardwalk. From the end of the boardwalk continue ahead through a gate, then a step stile in a collapsed wall.

2 Go half left (east) across a field to a gate giving access to a road. Cross the road to a signposted footpath, and use this for 150m/yds to Brackenbarrow Farm. There go through the gate on to a track enclosed by walls to continue through two more gates to a wooded path (signposted: Torver Common). Descend to a clearing on the shore of Coniston Water.

3 Turn right along the shore path, following it, first through woodland and then across open ground with steeply rising ground to your right. Keep going until your way is blocked by a wall. Bear right on an ascending path to a field gate, beyond which a track leads you to a road.

4 Turn right and follow the road, narrow in places and with no footpath, to the small village of Beckstones. Opposite the garage as you enter Beckstones, turn right into a small parking area to find a track on the left leading to a gate to Torver Common (signposted).

5 On the common, take the left hand track, which passes to the left of Kelly Hall Tarn, and stay with the track as it accompanies

a wall to a col overlooking Long Moss Tarn. Turn right on a path beside Long Moss, and at its end turn left to step across the outflow and so gain an undulating path heading north, later descending through juniper bushes to a gate. Continue now to the lake shore on a path through oak woodland, and at the shore turn left to a small gate.

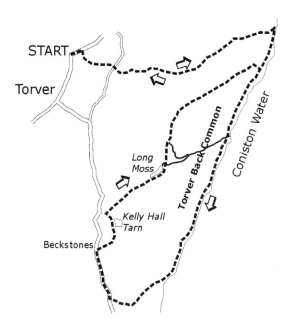

6 Walk on along a woodland path to the clearing encountered near the start of the walk, from where you can retrace your steps on a signposted woodland path, past Bracken Barrow to Torver.

14
Torver Low Common

An opportunity to get away from the crowds, over green paths and moorland used for centuries by farmers of Torver for the grazing of sheep and cattle. The land is now owned by the national park.

Start: Lay-by on A5084. GR288927

Total distance: 8.5 km (5¼ miles)

Height gain: 230m (755 feet)

Difficulty: Easy; some wet spots and a few unbridged streams. Not advised in poor visibility.

1 From the parking area cross the road and follow a signposted footpath through a gate, descending alongside a wall to cross Torver Beck by a wooden bridge. On a well-trodden path heading west, follow the course of Mire Beck for 600m/yds to a junction where you take the right hand fork to climb beside a tree-fringed gully to a small dam and reservoir.

2 From the dam take the path, right, first at the water's edge, but soon climbing to join a broad grassy track heading northeast. As you leave the reservoir behind the track descends, passing juniper bushes on the left, and then starts to climb to a grass-covered boulder. This boulder marks the start of a path going left (northwest), which you should follow. At first, as it crosses wet ground, it is indistinct, but improves as you go through bracken to a stream and a path junction.

3 Cross the stream and take a clear path to the left through dry bracken to a small tarn. Just before the tarn, go left, then right to circle round its head, over a col, then left along the line of a wall descending to a lane. Turn left along the lane, and climb steadily to a gate. Keep along the lane until you reach a sign directing you left on a cement track to Greaves Ground Farm.

4 From the farm gate the route is waymarked by yellow arrows, left, then right, through three gates to a track running alongside a wall. Keep with the track through yet another gate, across a patch of wet ground, then past a small, and often dry, tarn. Here the track swings, right, into a field, but you require a path climbing to the left (south) beside the wall. When the

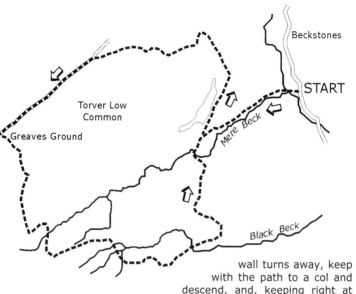

wall turns away, keep with the path to a col and descend, and, keeping right at the next junction, head for a small group of birch trees and a stream crossing.

5 After the stream, turn left on a narrow path alongside the boggy ground of Mere Moss to a small beck. Cross the beck to find a path running back to your right. Take this, back to the beck and a large yew tree, were the path turns to climb beside the beck in a shallow gully.

6 Near the top of the gully, the path climbs left to cross a col and descend between two small boulders on a green path through bracken.

7 At the end of the bracken follow its right hand edge round a small hill, then head for a solitary Scots pine, crossing a beck just before you reach the tree. Leave the tree, and pursue a clear path, first across a stream, and then round the base of a rocky outcrop to join a vehicle track heading northeast to a lane.

8 Turn left along the lane for 50m/yds to signposted track on the left. Follow the track to the dam and reservoir visited earlier. Take the descending path, right and follow it out to the Torver Beck bridge, and from there to the parking area.

15
Miners' Tracks
on Yewdale

This quiet walk follows green paths used by miners and quarrymen during the heyday of industrial activity among these southern fells of Lakeland.

Some of the tracks are now indistinct, and easy to miss, so be sure to chose a bright sunny day for a visit.

The splendid setting, amid gorse- and juniper-cloaked fellsides, must surely have lightened the burden of the hard-working quarrymen as they trudged wearily home at the end of their daily toil.

Start: Main car park, Coniston. GR303976

Total distance: 9km (5½ miles)

Height gain: 310m (1015 feet)

Difficulty: Moderate; mainly on open, bracken-clad fellsides, but not advised in poor visibility

1 Leave the car park and turn left, going past the church to a road junction. Turn right along the main road for a few strides to a lane on the left beside the Black Bull Inn. Take this lane heading out of the village, and at the end of the surfaced section turn right through a gate onto a green path with a wall on the right.

2 Continue to a wooden gate on the right, and there turn left on a narrow path climbing through bracken, gaining a little height to reach an oak tree. Take a moment to pause and admire the view over Coniston Water and the Yewdale Fells.

3 The way resumes by climbing through gorse bushes until the ground levels, joining a beck that leads you to a small tarn. Cross the beck at the tarn's outflow, and gain a little height to avoid wet ground. Look along the tarn for a cairn in a notch on the skyline, and head for it. From the cairn, your course is down the right-hand side of a wet grassy gully to another cairn at its base. Cross the gully, left, on to an indistinct grassy path,

Map labels:
Mines (Disused)

Crook Beck

Yewdale Fells

Miners' Bridge

Coniston

Dixon Ground

START

and shortly descend, right, to cross a beck and circle left round wet ground, to climb a grassy gully with a cairn visible at the top. From this fine vantage point you look out over the boggy expanse of Yewdale Crag Moss, with the dark crags of Wetherlam looming in the distance. Descend into a shallow dip from which cairns mark the path to a grassy ledge.

4 Turn left on a high path to another cairn. Turn right, and of the three paths then available to you, take the faint one on the right to descend a broad grassy ramp through bracken – the other two paths climb to higher ground, so ignore them.

5 As you descend, the path improves, with good views down the length of Yewdale and of Holme Fell across the valley. When you reach the head of a gill, the wet basin is circled left to gain a stone-edged track directly opposite. Ignore the well-worn path, right, into the gill, as it leads to the abrupt headwall of a quarry. Descend the stone-edged path through bracken and juniper-clad crags to bend right, following a beck to a path on the left.

6 Turn left, cross the beck, and climb to a col, there passing through the remains of a wall. Now descend on a path flanked by bracken to a small quarry hut. Turn left to pass a larger building and a tunnel into underground workings. Please note: This mine is still worked, and is not a place to explore.

7 Staying with the main track, descend to the road. Turn left along the road for 200m/yds to Tilberthwaite car park, and on approaching the car park take an ascending path on the left (signposted).

8 Go past the entrance to Penny Rigg Slate Quarry and continue climbing to a path junction beside the ruins of a quarry hut. Fork left on a rising path (the course of a water race from Crook Beck to Penny Rigg Mine), and follow the rim of Tilberthwaite Gill.

9 The path narrows and is exposed as it navigates around a small rocky side-stream. Proceed with caution on the path following the line of a water race, and traverse above the gorge to a path junction at Crook Beck. Do not cross the beck, but turn left and follow its right bank on a cairned path. Cross a stream above a beautiful rowan lined waterfall, and then climb steadily above the boggy wastes of Crook dam (now breached, but formerly supplying water to the Tilberthwaite workings below). Continue past a dangerous and flooded quarry to a small tarn at the head of the pass.

10 Cross the watershed and descend a dry grass gully, with the Old Man of Coniston directly ahead. The path bears left and descends in zigzags to the rear of a group of cottages (Irish Row). Keep with the main track. Turn left along Church Beck, and follow the track to a bridge over the beck. Immediately below the bridge a magnificent waterfall hides an old mine. Go down the track, over a cattle grid to the surfaced road by which you can easily return to Coniston.

16
Coniston to Torver

This easy walk makes use of the trackbed of the former Furness railway, returning on the high moorland packhorse trail of Walna Scar Road. The small village of Torver is Ideally-placed for a refreshment halt. Route-finding is clear throughout.

Start: Main car park, Coniston. GR303976

Total distance: 9.5 km (6 miles)

Height gain: 260m (855 feet)

Difficulty: Easy/Moderate; take care on the descending narrow road from Walna Scar to Coniston station.

1 Leave the car park and turn left, going past the church, then cross the bridge to turn right on a road leading past the Sun Hotel. The road climbs and zigzags, and at a T-junction, turn right, then left on a road passing small factory units and the Mountain Rescue Post. Keep on past a housing estate on the site of Coniston railway station. Follow the trackbed under the arch of a slate bridge and on to a gate spanning the track. Here a sign direct you to the road.

2 At the road, turn right, taking care against approaching traffic. After about 100m/yds, go left through a gate (signposted) on to a tree-lined track which leads down to the metalled access road to a caravan site. Keep going (southwest) along the road until it turns right. Here continue ahead on a track through trees to a wall blocking the track. At the wall turn left, through a gate, then by a grass track, keeping to the base of rising ground on your right. Bear right and follow the track across a beck to a ladder stile over a wall.

3 Over the stile, a gated track through trees leads you to a gate beyond which the track goes left across the top of a field. Keeping a head on your right, go past a gate and cattle grid to a field gate into the yard of Hoathwaite Farm.

4 Enter the yard and turn right at a signed opening between buildings to pass through sheep pens into a field, then keeping to the fence to a field gate.

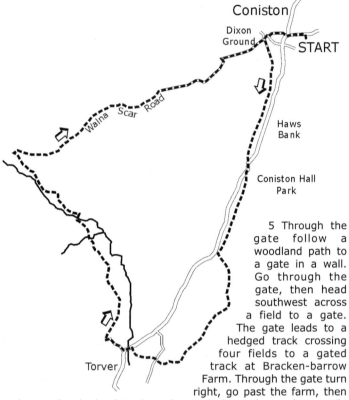

5 Through the gate follow a woodland path to a gate in a wall. Go through the gate, then head southwest across a field to a gate. The gate leads to a hedged track crossing four fields to a gated track at Bracken-barrow Farm. Through the gate turn right, go past the farm, then by another hedged track to the road. Cross the road to a stile and head west across fields to the old railway track and a road.

6 Turn left along the road to a signposted bridleway on the right.

If you wish to depart from the walk for a moment, you can go down to Torver for refreshments. Otherwise...

7 Turn right and follow a waymarked track through the village of Scar Head to join a walled bridleway. At the third gate, continue ahead across a bridge over Tranearth Beck on to a rough track leading to a gated sheep pen. Follow waymarks through the pen to a wooden bridge over Torver Beck, cross the bridge and turn left towards Bannishead Quarry.

8 Now follow the fence, right, to take an ascending terraced path beside the beck, heading for a large cairn on the Walna Scar Road. At the cairn, turn right, and descend between rock cuttings on a clear track heading northeast over open fellside, passing reed-filled Boo Tarn en route. The road runs down to a parking area on the right, and a gate at the top of a metalled roadway.

Go through the gate and, with care, follow the ensuing narrow road beck to Coniston.

Along the way

Furness Railway The Furness Railway Cokpany opened the branch line from Foxfield to Coniston in 1859 to carry copper ore and slate from the mines to the coastal port of Greenodd.

John Ruskin opposed the railway when it was first proposed, but when the line was finally laid, it was skilfully screened by trees and rock cuttings.

With the decline of mining and the quarry industry, and the lack of passenger traffic, the line closed in October 1985. Since then the station has been developed for housing and small workshops.

Commons

Commons are areas of open land in England and Wales over which adjoining owners and occupiers have certain rights 'in common' with each other. Formerly, commons used to be the wastelands of medieval manors, and those enjoying rights over them - the 'commoners' - were invariably tenants of the lord of the manor.

The principal rights were pasturage, the right to graze cattle (known as 'pannage' in the case of swine), piscary (the right to fish), turbary (the right to dig turf), and estovers (the right to take wood for repairs or firewood).

17
Rose Castle
and Sawrey Ground

This pleasant walk starts along the shore of Tarn Hows, soon leaving this popular visitor location and passing the small Lakeland cottage of 'Rose Castle', with its unusual arched windows and more traditional round chimney. Little-visited field paths with splendid views of surrounding fells, lead a return through the grounds of Sawrey Ground and Hill Fell plantation.

Start: National Trust car park, Tarn Hows. GR326995

Total distance: 4km (2½ miles)

Height gain: 129m (421feet)

Difficulty: An easy walk, on well-maintained paths near the tarns on to field paths, which can be wet in places. The final section from Sawrey Ground has a rough and stony ascent

1 Leave the car park by the entrance to walk around the tarn, cross the road and descend towards the gate at the tarn dam. Before the gate, turn right on a path along the tarn edge to a T-junction.

2 Here go left for 100m/yds, through a gate and continue for 500m/yds with splendid views over the tarn of the Langdale Pikes. Shortly after passing the second seat take a gated track back right, (signposted Hawkshead).

3 Ascending to a T-junction, turn left along a broad track to a small cottage (Rose Castle). Going past the cottage the path curves to the right (waymarked) to gain a green trod. Keeping the wall below to the left go over the step stile into woodland.

4 In the woodland cross a track and go alongside the remains of a wall to a gate. Through this gate with wall and woodland to your right, head for another gate to gain a walled track. Descend the enclosed track through the next gate, and then follow the road between buildings to gain a tarmac access lane, accompany this to the main road.

5 At the road junction cross the cattle grid and use a field gate

on the right to gain a footpath (signposted; Sawrey
Ground). Proceed across the
field making for a stand of
pines in the far corner and a **START**
step stile into the garden of
Sawrey Ground. Keep to the
marked path through the
garden to cross a stile to a
parking area and tarmac
drive, then walk along the
drive to the road.

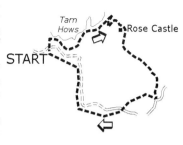

This road is narrow and the main vehicle route to Tarn Hows

Keep children under close supervision.

6 Go left along the road for 100m/yds and take the gated
footpath on the right (Signposted; Tarn Hows). Through the
gate turn right on a clear path and ascend to a wall junction,
here take the path right, signed. To the tarns, keep the fence
on your right go past one gate and ascend to the next gate at
the road. Do not go through this gate but turn left alongside the
wall (way marked), past the next gate to a fourth one.

7 Use this gate to gain the road, turn left and at the end of the
wall on the left side take a grassy trod leading to the car park
or go right across the road to the tarn.

Along the way

Rose Castle With such a grand name, you would be forgiven
for thinking that this dwelling was a large commanding
building. In fact, Rose Castle is a small slate cottage with
striking arched windows and traditional round Lakeland chimney. Part of the Monk Coniston Estate, the cottage was most
likely used by workers in the near by quarries.

In 1930 Mrs William Heelis, (better known as Beatrix Potter),
bought the estate. She sold half of the estate to the National
Trust and bequeathed it the other half. She also, for the
remainder of her life, acted as land agent for the trust. In a
letter to Mr S H Hamer in 1931, she complained of the condition
of Rose Castle and the possibility of trouble if the sanitary
inspector were to find it in this condition: 'Talk of over-
crowding in a slum. There are 8 beds in a small chamber,
formerly servant's bedroom with one narrow window, much
tighter packed than Far End cows.'

18
Hill Fell Plantation and Wharton Tarn

During the 19th century James Marshall of Monk Coniston, planted vast areas of the estate with large pines from North America. On this walk through Hill Fell Plantation the splendour of many of these pines can be seen. The National Trust now manage the plantation both for our enjoyment and for timber crops used elsewhere on the estate.

Start: National Trust car park, Tarn Hows GR326995

Total distance: 3.2km (2 miles)

Height gain: 117m (385 feet)

Difficulty: Easy; on woodland tracks and paths, with a short wet section near Wharton Tarn.

1 From the pedestrian exit of the car park take the signposted path back and right through birch trees, above the parking area to a gate. Go through the gate to access Hill Fell Plantation, and descend a broad track through mixed woodland to a bend left, then right, over a stream to a T-junction.

2 Turn right signposted; Boon Crag, Coniston) continue for 100m/yds with stream on your right to the next junction. Keep to the left (signposted: Hollin Bank, Wharton Tarn), now with a fence on the right pass the next track left and proceed for 200m/yds. As the track curves left take the left branch at the next junction signed 'Wharton Tarn'.

3 You will then climb to a gated deer fence. Through the gate, keep with the track and descend through spruce and birch trees to a way marked path on the left.

4 Go along this woodland path, and then beside Wharton Tarn, this section is boggy in places, to another deer fence. Through

the gate keep with the waymarked path to the next gated fence.

5 Here, do not use the gate, but instead turn left along side the fence on an ascending path to the road. At the road go left (way marked) by a wall, past the next gate to a third gate.

6 Use this gate to gain the road, turn left a few metres, then take the green trod left and return to the car park.

Grisedale Forest

The woodlands of Monk Coniston Moor, along with many other properties, were acquired by the Forestry Commission in 1934 to create the larger Grisedale Forest. The forest contains not only large tracts of conifer but also areas of oak coppice dating from the 16th and 17th centuries, and supporting communities of wild life, including both red and roe deer.

The moorland sheep grazings of Lawson Park, a monastic sheep farm dating from medieval times, and desperately over-grzed, are now planted with larch.

Brantwood

The whole area around Coniston is associated with John Ruskin, who lived until his death at Brantwood above the shores of Coniston Water.

When Ruskin bought Brantwood in 1871 the house was half the size it is today. The original house was a modest six or eight-roomed villa, built at the end of the 18th century by Thomas Woodville. Ruskin bought the freehold of Brantwood for the sum of £1,500. He knew Coniston and while never seeing the interior of Brantwood he was familiar with the property and thought that any house opposite Coniston Old Man 'must be beautiful'.

19
Blawith Common

Situated to the south of Coniston, Blawith Common is pleasantly remote from the main walking areas of Lakeland. This has the compensation of exploring an area rich in the flora and bird life that are now hard to find in parts which are more popular.

The common was once richly wooded and supplied the bloomeries of Coniston in medieval times for smelting iron ore. It was later cleared for sheep grazing, and makes for an ideal introduction to walking in rough country for children.

Kept for a clear day the reward from the Beacon, the highest point of the common, are splendid views of the Coniston Fells and the surrounding area.

Start: Brown Howe, car park and picnic area. GR290910

Total distance: 6.8 km (4½ miles)

Height gain: 282m (925 feet)

Difficulty: A rewarding walk, on good fell paths that can be wet in places especially near Beacon Tarn.

Not to be tackled in poor visibility.

1 Leave the car park and go left along the road for 100m/yds to a tarmac lane on the right. Take this lane climbing steeply at first fringed by birch, alder and juniper, later by bracken and bog myrtle.

2 Pass a signposted footpath on the left and continue soon to accompany a wall for a short distance. 150m/yds after the wall falls away to the right, look for a path to the left at a right-hand bend.

3 Take this path, first over a grassy mound to a small stream. Cross the stream, go left on a well-trodden path to a T-junction, and turn right. A steady climb through bracken leads to a col, some boggy ground and a small reed-filled tarn.

4 A small cairn to the left marks the start of a higher path between small boulders above the wet ground. At the end of the boggy area a short climb leads to a shallow col, over which Beacon Tarn comes into view.

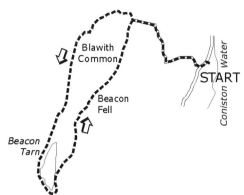

5 Descend towards the tarn, at a fork junction take the path right, now with the tarn below to your left walk along this path, wet in places, passing a small stand of pine and chestnut trees to the tarn outflow.

6 Cross the outflow by stepping-stones and keep left by the tarn shore for 200m/yds to a broad green path climbing to the right. Take this path and as it descends to a large boulder go right on an ascending path, then climb right, over a small rocky outcrop and continue on a grassy trod between boulders. As Coniston Water comes into view look for the summit cairn to your left.

7 From the summit return to the main path, go to your left and descend on a clear broad path, first with heather and bilberry, but later bracken. Keep with this path ignoring other paths left or right. Pass under power cables and then accompany a small stream through a stand of oak trees to reach the lane, turn right and retrace your steps to the car park.

Blawith

Blawith is a collection of farms and cottages, at the southern end of Coniston Water, near the River Crake. Blawith Common there was once a prehistoric settlement.

The common is a large expanse of wild and craggy moorland rich in archaeological sites. Blawith is pronounced Blaith, meaning a wolf, which were once common in the area.

20
Yewdale Circuit

Most of Yewdale and its farms formed part of the Monk Coniston Estate, which Mrs William Heelis (Beatrix Potter) purchased in 1930 and bequeathed to the National Trust on her death.

In spring and early summer, the field meadows are awash with wild flowers and old woodland floors are coated in bluebells.

A most unusual dog kennel is passed on the route, as is Yew Tree Farm with its distinctive 'spinning gallery', where depending on the working of the farm, it is possible to be served refreshments.

Start: Parking area on the road to Hodge Close, near Shepherd's Bridge. GR314998

Total distance: 6.7km (4¼ miles)

Height gain: 259m (850 feet)

Difficulty: Moderate/Easy; on well-maintained paths. A short section along a main road and crossing the main Coniston to Ambleside road near the end.

1 From the parking area go left along the bridleway signposted for Coniston. Keep with this path through a gate then beside the main road to a side turning to Tilberthwaite. Cross the side road to a path into woodland (Great Intake), continue on this woodland path for 1.7km (1 mile) to the second exit to the road.

2 Bear right for 50m/yds to a gate, pass through and keep the wall to your left for 200m/yds to another gate on the left. Going through this gate, pass between houses to gain a tarmac lane and turn right past the YHA to a junction at the main road.

3 Crossing over this main road, then walk along the road opposite, signed Hawkshead for 300m/yds to the primary School, here take the signposted, footpath left over a bridge (Shepherd Bridge). Across the bridge go left over a step stile, then by a waymarked path through a gate to gain a well-trodden field path. Keep with this path at first over open ground, then alongside a fence to a gate near a building (Dog Kennel Folly).

4 Pass through the gate, taking time to investigate this unusual building. Then the onward route is again on a well-trodden path climbing with a fence to your right to a gate, through which continue for 100m/yds until the wall to your right falls away. Here bear right on a path between the wall and gorse bushes, at end of the bushes go left to cross a wet area on broad walks and then climb to a gateway into High Guards and Guards Wood.

5 In the woodland, keep to the waymarked path, at first climbing in pine plantation, but after passing through a fallen wall descend through broadleaved woodland with views of Coniston Water. Leave the woodland via a field gate and use the broad track to another gate to a lane. Go left, signposted Low Yewdale, for 50m/yds to a gate on the right, waymarked footpath.

6 Use the gate to gain a broad track and climb to a second gate, going through this the track continues below a stand of beech trees, as it follows the line of trees look over and climb to a gate in the fence to your right. Through this gate keep to the green trod alongside Tarn Hows Wood to a gate leading to the access lane to Tarn Hows Cottage.

7 Cross the access lane and with the perimeter wall of the cottage grounds to your left descend to a small gate, through which go right by the fence to a step-stile. Over the stile, bear left alongside a wall, then right past a large beech tree (fenced) to a gate leading to the main road (A593). Cross the road and use the access to Yew Tree Farm to gain a gated track near the main farm

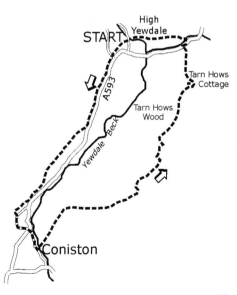

gate. Climb in zigzags to a second gate, through which bear left alongside a wall and continue on a grass track through three more gates until arriving at a gate at the road to Hodge Close, cross the bridge spanning Yewdale Beck to return to the parking area.

Along the way

Dog Kennel Folly Built during the 19th century when the Victorians had a passion for disguising buildings so that they appeared more grand than they really were, this folly was built as a dog kennel by James Marshall of Monk Coniston for his pack of fox hounds. Now in the care of the National Trust, the building has been restored after a major collapse in the mid-1990s.

Yew Tree Farm As part of the Monk Coniston Estate, the farm was purchased in 1930 by Mrs William Heelis and on her death inherited by the National Trust. Built in the 17th century the cruck-framed farmhouse, named after a large Yew Tree that was felled in 1896 and was said to be 700 years old.

During the economic hard time of the 1930s Mrs Heelis encouraged her tenants to welcome visitors. At her own expense, she helped tenants in setting up small tearooms with furniture she bought at local sales.

The present tenants of the farm once again offer afternoon teas to passing walkers, but this does depend on the time of year and the workings of the farm.

QUESTA PUBLISHING

WALKS WITH CHILDREN

LAKE DISTRICT
Borrowdale
Buttermere and the Vale of Lorton
Around Coniston
Keswick and the Newlands Valley
Around Ambleside and Grasmere
Ullswater
Around Kendal
Around Windermere
South Lakeland

YORKSHIRE DALES
Wharfedale
Swaledale
Wensleydale

PEAK DISTRICT
Dark Peak

also

SHORT WALKS IN THE EDEN VALLEY & NORTH PENNINES

All QUESTA titles
are available from
PO BOX 520, BAMBER BRIDGE, PRESTON,
LANCASHIRE PR5 8LF

or by FAX to
0870 137 8888
Website: www.questapublishing.co.uk